hamburger
汉堡包 hànbǎobāo

sandwich
sānmíngzhì

chicken
鸡 jī 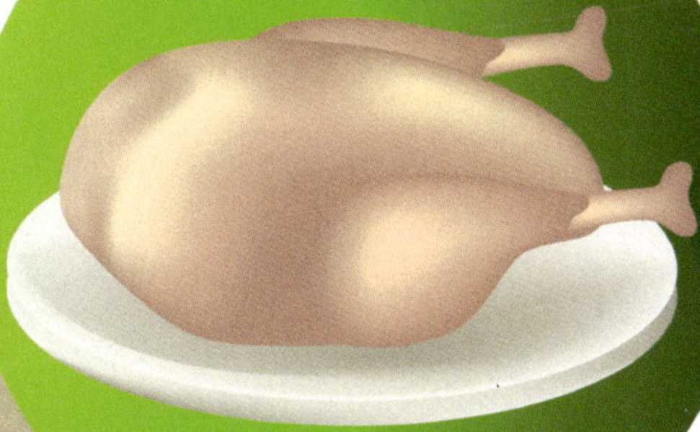

egg
鸡蛋 jīdàn

spaghetti
意大利面 yì dà lì miàn

pizza
比萨 bǐsà

SHAPES

形状
xíngzhuàng

circle

圆形
yuán xíng

rectangle

长方形
chángfāngxíng

square

正方形
zhèngfāngxíng

Disclaimer: Copyright© 2018 Jane Thai Little Yapper Press. All rights reserved. No part of this publication may be reproduced, replicated, distributed or transmitted in any form or by any means including electronic or mechanical photocopying, recording, or any information storage or retrieval system, without prior written permission from the publisher.

Purpose: The purpose of this book is to provide basic reading for children ages 1 and up. Please feel free to contact me at littleyapperbooks@gmail.com for comments.

About the author: Jane is an author, designer and educator. These days, you will find her drawing and writing children's books. She draws her inspiration from her students and her daughter. Jane lives in the Big Apple with her husband, daughter and beloved yorkies.

Author Page: www.amazon.com/author/janethai

Dedication: In memory of Forrest & Mocha Lee

I belong to:

Author's Notes

Help your child begin and build their first words in Chinese. This easy to follow picture word book is written in both English and simplified Chinese. Children learn best with visuals and can be taught to be bilingual at a very young age. In fact it is recommended that they learn another language as early as possible. This book contains many everyday objects and animals that children will see. Help your child reinforce vocabulary by pointing to real life objects at home or anywhere else.
If you do not speak Chinese, you can still teach your child and give them a starting foundation to work with. Audio files of this book can be downloaded free with purchase of book at littleyapper.com. Have fun learning together!

Learn more about how to teach your child a second language at littleyapper.com.

LIVE & LEARN

FIRST WORDS IN CHINESE

中文 的 第一批 词语
zhōngwén de dì yī pī cí yǔ

Numbers

数字
shùzì

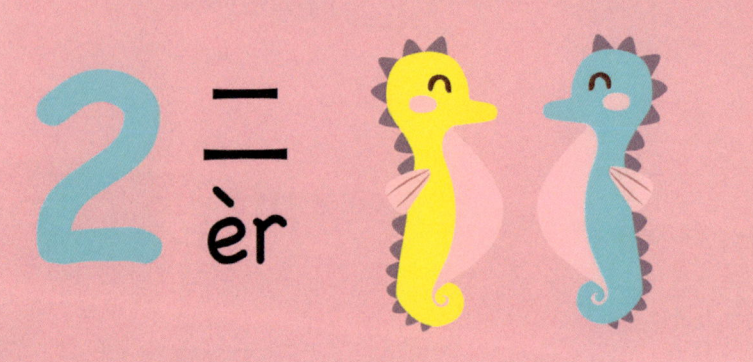

1 一 yī

2 二 èr

3 三 sān

4 四 sì

5 五 wǔ

6 六 liù

7 七 qī

8 八 bā

9 九 jiǔ

10 十 shí

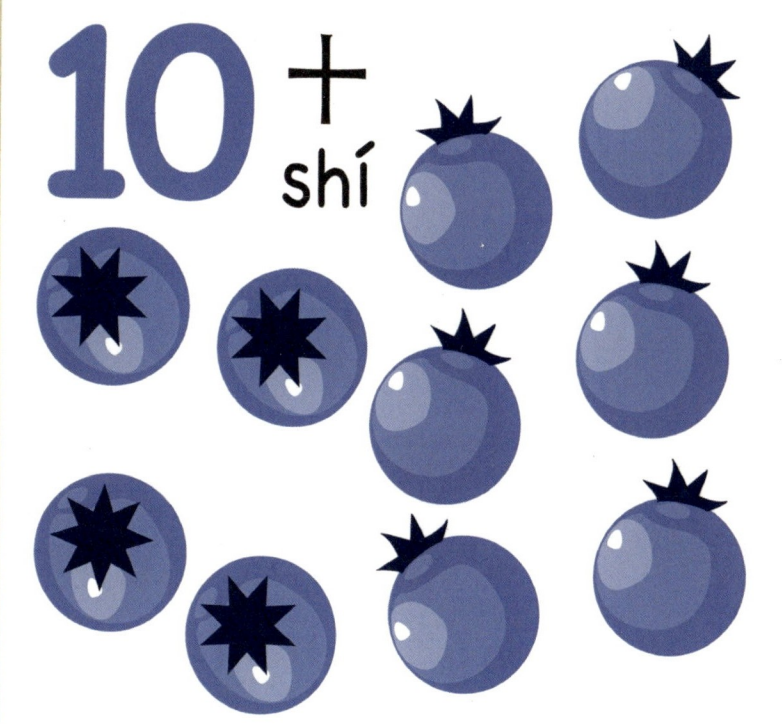

COLORS
颜色
yán sè

red — 红色 hóng sè

yellow — 黄色 huáng sè

brown — 棕色 zōng sè

black — 黑色 hēi sè

purple — 紫色 zǐ sè

蓝色 lán sè	绿色 lǜ sè	白色 bái sè
橙色 chéng sè	粉红色 fěnhóng sè	灰色 huī sè

PETS
宠物
chǒngwù

hamster
仓鼠
cāngshǔ

chameleon
变色龙
biànsèlóng

fish 鱼
yú

turtle

乌龟
wūguī

parrot

鹦鹉
yīngwǔ

cat

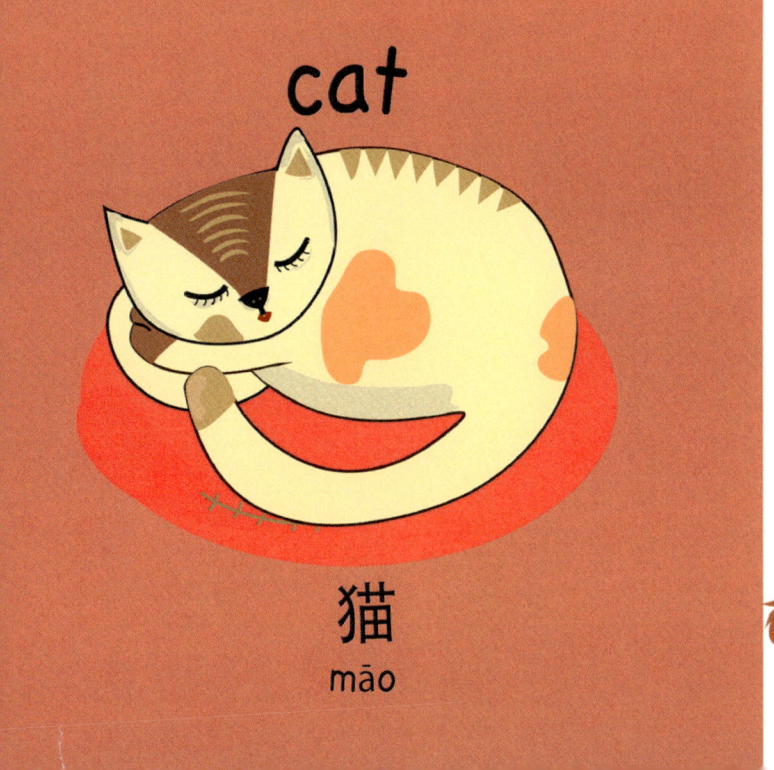

猫
māo

dog

狗
gǒu

FRUITS
水果 shuǐguǒ

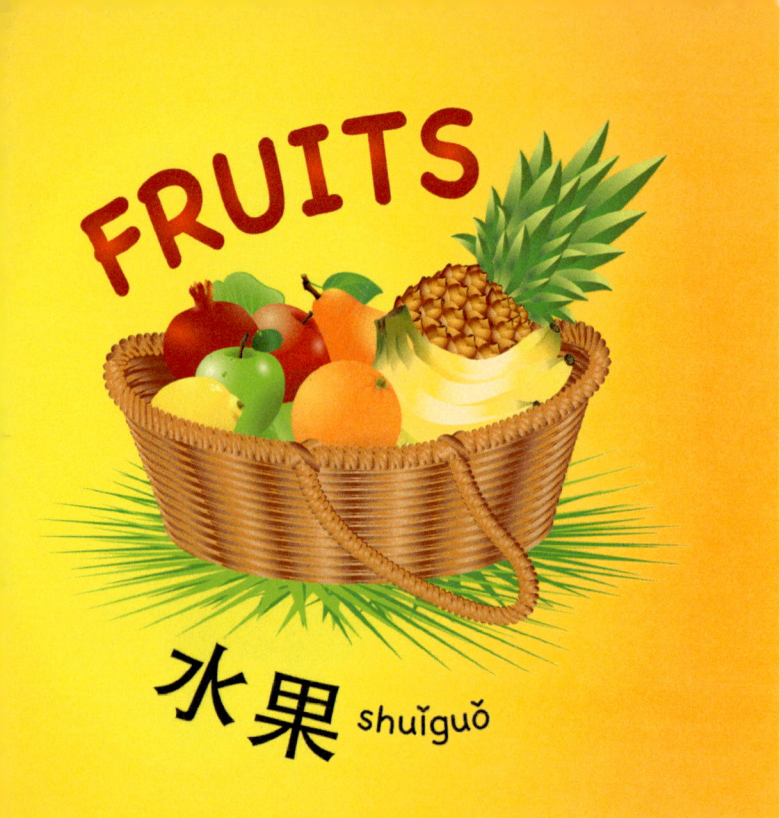

grape
葡萄 pútáo

blueberry
蓝莓 lánméi

pear
梨 lí

orange
桔子 júzi

lemon
柠檬 níngméng

pineapple
菠萝
bōluó

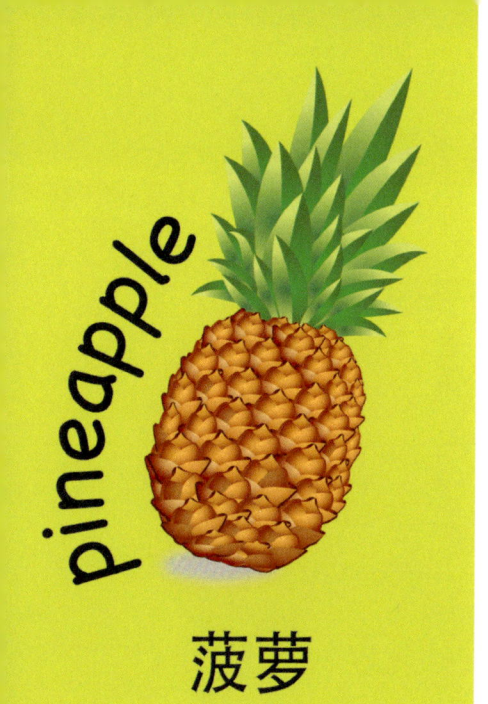

banana
香蕉
xiāngjiāo

strawberry
草莓
cǎoméi

watermelon
西瓜
xīguā

apple
苹果 
píngguǒ

Vegetables

蔬菜
shūcài

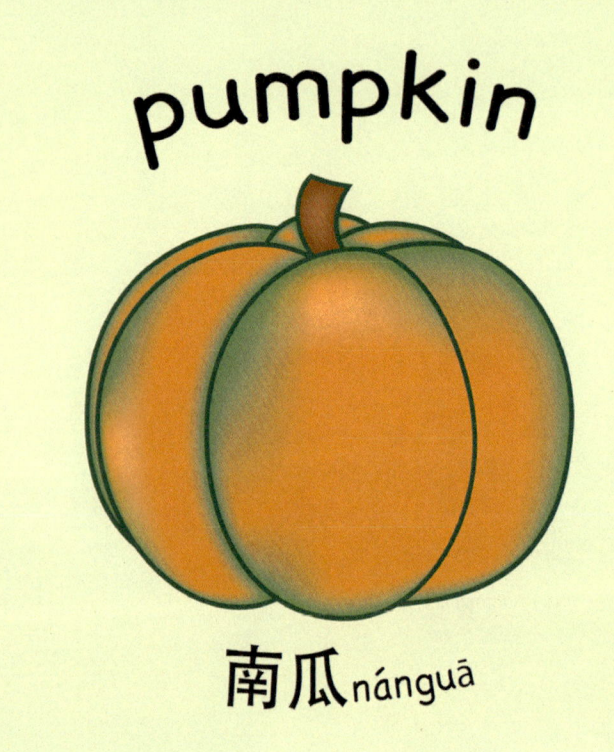

pumpkin
南瓜 nánguā

onion
洋葱
yángcōng

carrot
胡萝卜 húluóbo

lettuce
生菜
shēngcài

corn
玉米
yùmǐ

turnip
萝卜
luóbo

cucumber
黄瓜
huángguā

broccoli
西兰花
xīlánhuā

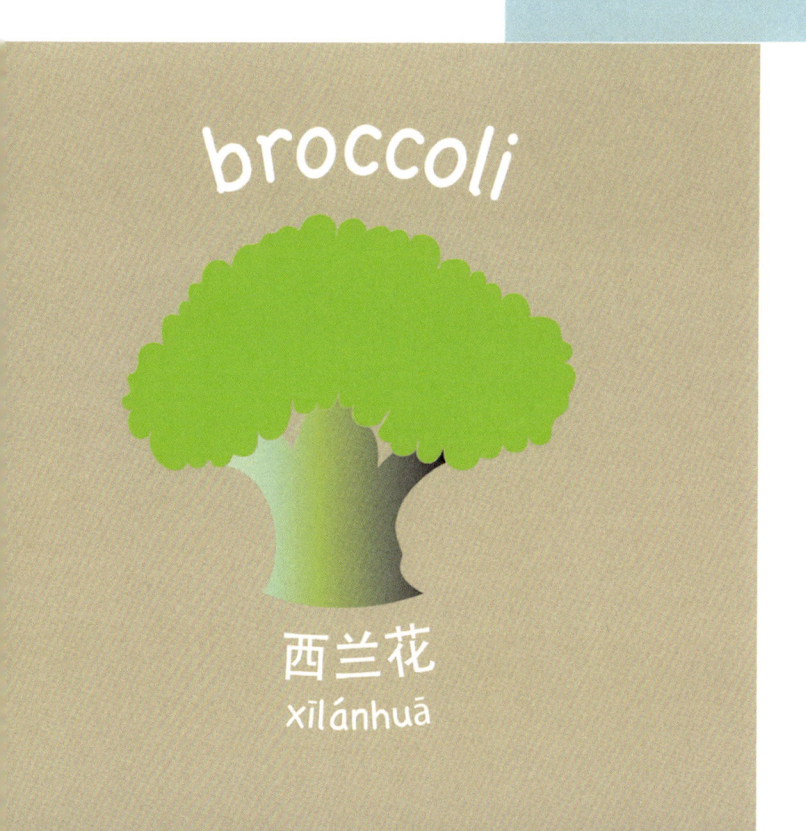

eggplant
茄子
qiézi

Food 食品
shípǐn

bread

面包
miànbāo

cookies

饼干
bǐnggān

cheese 奶酪
nǎilào

chocolate

巧克力
qiǎokèlì

pie

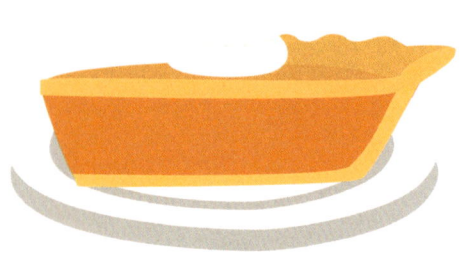

派
pài

hamburger
汉堡包 hànbǎobāo

sandwich 三明治
sānmíngzhì

chicken
鸡 jī 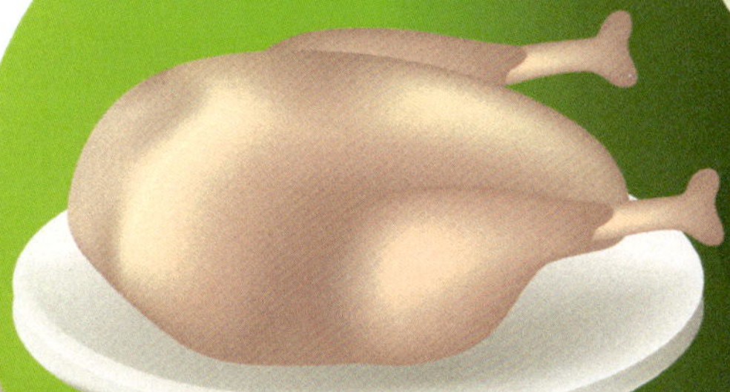

egg
鸡蛋 jīdàn

spaghetti
意大利面 yì dà lì miàn

pizza
比萨 bǐsà

SHAPES

形状
xíngzhuàng

circle
圆形
yuán xíng

rectangle
长方形
chángfāngxíng

square
正方形
zhèngfāngxíng

oval

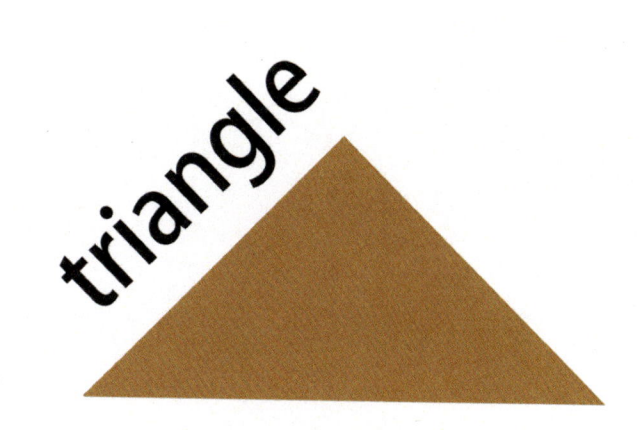

椭圆形
tuǒyuán xíng

heart

心形
xīn xíng

triangle

三角形
sānjiǎoxíng

star

星形
xīng xíng

instruments
乐器
yuèqì

violin
小提琴
xiǎotíqín

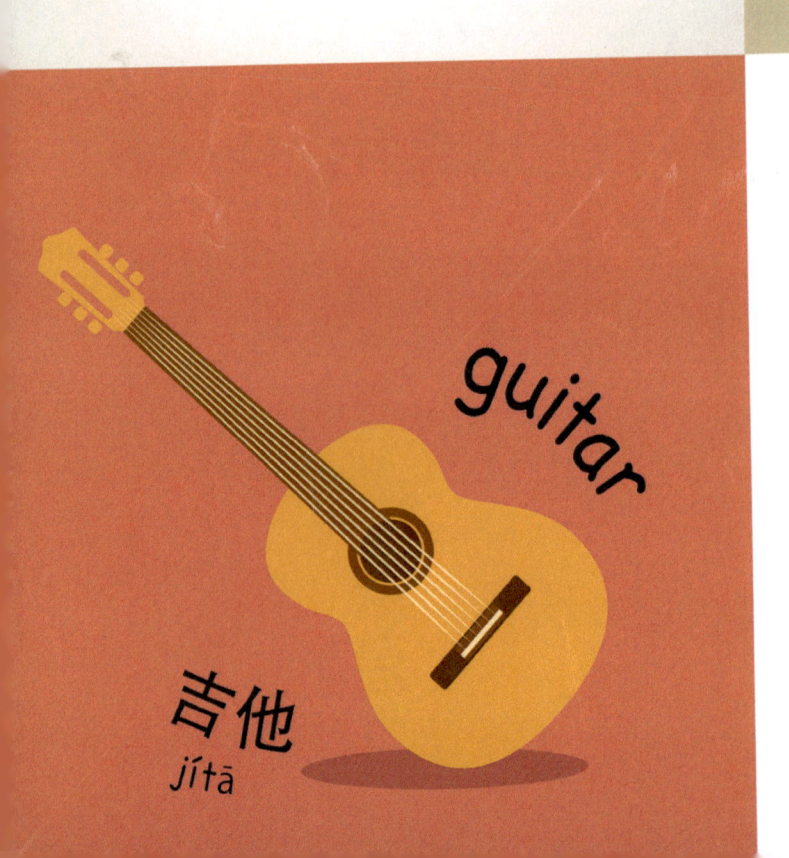

guitar
吉他
jítā

piano
钢琴
gāngqín

maracas
马拉卡斯
mǎ lā kǎ sī

saxophone
萨克思风
sà kè sī fēng

tambourine
手鼓 shǒugǔ

drum
鼓
gǔ

Transportation

交通工具
jiāotōng gōngjù

bicycle
自行车
zìxíngchē

car 汽车
qìchē

boat 船 chuán

submarine
潜艇 qiántǐng

school bus 校车
xiàochē

ambulance 救护车
jiùhù chē

air balloon
气球
qìqiú

airplane
飞机
fēijī

motorcycle
摩托车
mótuō chē

train 火车
huǒchē

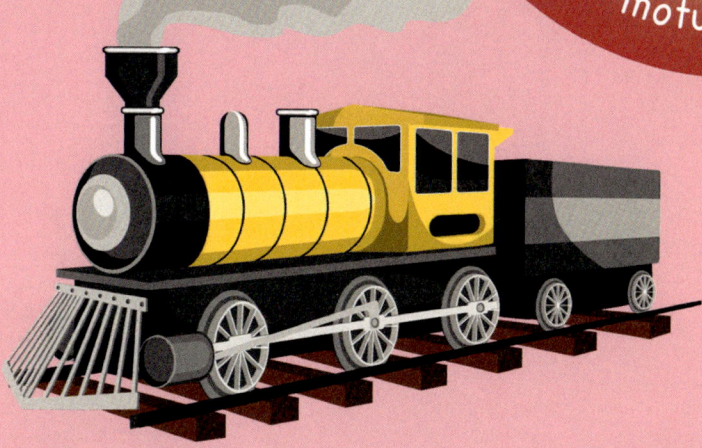

truck 卡车
kǎchē

Wild Animals
野生动物
yěshēng dòngwù

bat
蝙蝠 biānfú

alligator
鳄鱼 èyú

zebra
斑马 bānmǎ

hippopotamus
河马 hémǎ

raccoon
狸
lí

ostrich
鸵鸟
tuóniǎo

gorilla
大猩猩
dà xīngxīng

ram
公羊
gōng yáng

Sea Animals
海洋动物
hǎiyáng dòngwù

seahorse — 海马 hǎimǎ

sea turtle — 海龟 hǎiguī

fish — 鱼 yú

sea star — 海星 hǎixīng

eel — 鳗鱼 mányú

jellyfish — 海蜇 hǎizhé

crab 螃蟹 pángxiè

dolphin 海豚 hǎitún

clam 蛤蜊 gélí

whale 鲸鱼 jīngyú

octopus 章鱼 zhāngyú

OBJECTS 物
wù

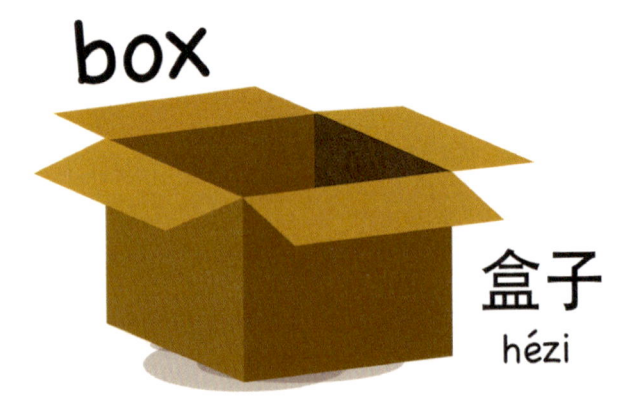

box
盒子 hézi

pencils
铅笔 qiānbǐ

toy bear
玩具熊 wánjù xióng

umbrella
雨伞 yǔsǎn

scissor

剪刀
jiǎndāo

basketball

篮球
lánqiú

books

书
shū

clock

时钟 shízhōng

Clothing
衣服
yīfú

shirt
衬衫
chènshān

pajamas
睡衣
shuìyī

underwear
内裤
nèikù

socks
袜子
wàzi

coat
外套
wàitào

- dress — 连衣裙 liányīqún
- sweater — 毛衣 máoyī
- pants — 裤子 kùzi
- mittens — 手套 shǒutào
- scarf — 围巾 wéijīn
- hat — 帽子 màozi
- shoes — 鞋子 xiézi

THE END

故事结束
gùshì jiéshù

If you have enjoyed this book, please share and leave me a comment at **littleyapper.com**. A review on Amazon.com would be appreciated as well.
Thank you. 谢谢

Use code : **FIRSTWORDS** to download your FREE audio book and find out more tips on dual language learning at **littleyapper.com**

Other dual language books by Jane Thai

The Apple Tree
How Mommy Carries Her Baby
How the World got its Color from the Sea
12 Months of the Year
I like Pickles